1 . iv. MMXI

The English Sweats
James Brookes

for Sarah

at Hawthornden

from James,

ISBN 978-1-906309-10-7

First published December 2009 by

Pighog Press
PO Box 145
Brighton BN1 6YU
England UK

info@pighog.co.uk

www.pighog.co.uk

Twitter www.twitter.com/pighog

Design by Curious
www.curiouslondon.com

for Des, Betty, Stan and Lee

Caractacus ... wandered about the city after his liberation; and after beholding its splendour and its magnitude he exclaimed: "And can you, then, who have such possessions and so many of them, covet our poor tents?"

Cassius Dio, Roman History: Epitome of Book LXI

Contents

Portents

cui candor morte redemptus

caption to Henry Peacham's *Emblem* 75

The week stoat turned to ermine,
it entered our houses:
this wasting illness.

Too proud from the offing
we went by the old signs:
civet and leeches,

phrenology, dowsing.
The fever still came on:
it broke our houses;

we were a client kingdom.
We turned at bay then:
we wove *isti mirant*.

'Who now is our vicegerent?'
we ask, half-despairing,
clinging to relics

precision-tooled, imported
from Arimathea,
things snuck through customs:

the twice-flowering hawthorn
and a bowl for bleeding:
a needful foreign

body, a fleam, a lancet,
the spear of Longinus.

Shrike

Call a harsh 'chack'; song is a scratchy warble
catching my origins in a thicket of oak.
My passerine tact a mystery to the hawk.
A week in my wingspan is idle flit and hack;
my back's bitter blood-bolt, the terse use of my beak
to keep my barbed-wire larder of corpses in stock.
No carrion-charmer, no falcon or red kite
I, peregrine, I pious in thought and act
am shriven in my little blood, my butcher's reek.
In the wrack of my nest, in its bone-scree of voles and shrews
I am called to the questing retch of my home choir.
Their eyrie-cry my *kyrie eleison.*

Requiem for an Invasion

The dice of drowned men's bones he saw bequeath
An embassy

Hart Crane

By freight going landward,
our half of the *Mary Rose*,
sleeping through polyphonies of weather.

A hand snagged in the water.
Trowels and airlifts and gently wafting silt.
Whorled, our native churchyard verdigris,
across the steeps
of chalk-familiar cloud, the hills of samphire.

Up, up we went, through the cleft of marriage,
as though it needed to take
only our arms past the elbow, to lift and salvage.

When did the clutch-bone current find us out?
Loved enemy, let
our ribs slant and meet
as fingers at prayer
our hearts a tumbled brace of Whitby jet.

The Crescent of Hearing

1587

You hear tides. Where the tale outwears the teller
is a wide turn, slow at the tiller.
Good news travels slower,

not a rainbow portrait, not all ears.
Each new gust of the swelling cheek
blows scattered rumour,

leaves the listener drydocked: the Duke of Parma's
troops idling in Dunkirk, Medina Sedona's
crescent of ships at anchor.

Fear's a great converser. Pass it on,
tongue-heavy, pendant, thin as bell's bronze
gone chap-worn, after a year of terrors.

Or later, wonders, jetsam with such details
as neeptide doubloons shingling Donegal

1637

The Archbishop of Canterbury, being informed by his spies
what Mr Prynne said, moved the Lords then sitting
in the Star Chamber that he might be gagged
and have some further censure to be presently
executed on him; but that motion did not succeed.
Mr Burton spake much while in the pillory to the people.
The executioner cut off his ears deep and close,
in a cruel manner, with much effusion of blood,
an artery being cut, as there was likewise of Dr Bastwick.
Then Mr Prynne's cheeks were seared with an iron
made exceeding hot; which done, the executioner
cut off one of his ears and a piece of his cheek
with it; then hacking the other ear almost off,
he left it hanging and went down; but being called
up again he cut it quite off.

1737

A shrivelled *casus belli* in the Commons,
the boxed once-ear of Captain Jenkins
is seven years of cartilage and pickle.
Like snuff or contraband, like a bad joke
this dumb witness passes round the Frontbench.
The Speaker puts the question, the tellers count.

1937

Tintin searches for the broken eared fetish,

ends up in San Theodoros as a colonel
[3487 colonels
        but only 49 corporals in that army].
Promise of quarantine
        for aggressor nations,
a bullet
        for the last Balinese tiger.
Toscanini's   Christmas;
        peaceful radio

Ivor Gurney dies, speaking to Schubert.

Badger

Bitumen dog, dock-tailed, huge on the loose,
full contact ash-scuttle head and shovel-brow,
tilting its panzerfaust snout, scrounge-clad
in Angevin scrubbed velvet; 1/34th scale
S-P artillery at large in Sussex, flanks
all hugger-mugger with the undergrowth.
Alive, gone tumour-mad, fleeing the cull
of its own acute senses; tight muzzle
knowing its own tagged conservation zone
for every groped root and whiff of fox-piss
and that last feral part that must shunt
hard-shoulder for tubercular lebensraum.

Crept back exhausted, habits documented
by faecal distribution and content.
Deaf from his hard-breathing
echoes. His overdug sett.
The expectation of his
rutting and rearing.
Weald weary,
blown.

Barn Conversion

It was this night I believe...that I saw the impossibility of staying in the Church of England.

Gerard Manley Hopkins, journal entry June 17th 1866

The final fifty miles to Horsham
break you in each stride, ruin the hems
of all your best coats, trudging through the loam.
Heels red-raw, soles worn so thin the ground
is hurt incarnate, so when at last you find the barn
not even halting halts the steady burn.

To know this weariness not even half-way home –
you didn't pay the rent boy – out you're turned,
a squatter, refused usucaption.
Time to receive the pent-up Kingdom Come.
Kneel down.

The English Sweats

Laid out in the field
is a Doomsday town
depopulated by *sudor anglicus.*

And up on the hill
past the rectory
the heir looks up his marriage in Debrett's:

the year that he learnt
the bark of muntjac
mating or birthing from the scream of a child;

to tell the marquee
and the caterers' van
from the unmarked car and the white tent rising.

Sometimes in his dreams
his father's spirit
caught by the creeping terror of the 'new build',

shows him a pistol
kept in the desk drawer
to plug his Château Pétrus with dum-dum rounds

or his grandfather
still coming for him
on a transport ship from the pas-de-Calais,

 wrists bound saltire-wise
to the ensign pole,
ankles drumming their tattoo on the transom.

Recently Sighted

A mollusc, a Spiny Dye
Murex, whose name might be Poins or Peto.
One in the hotel lobby,
slouching; maybe someone you used to know.

Aspirations: a purple pinstripe; press
attention (gloss or greyscale). At risk from:
saline; Myrmidons' widows; cosh-
or garrotte-savvy thugs. Distribution:

first floor victim of a pyramid scam;
children's entertainer on a cross
channel ferry (Dover to Rotterdam).

Habitat: the bar's side of the dance-floor
Ridens poculum sorpilo sputis bibens
(that is: smiling, tilting a cuspidor).

Mons Horse Burial

Haunch of a 13-pounder, mud-locked. One pelvic wheel.
The barrel down-tilt, something of a horse
straddling it. At half dismount
the trooper, dirigible angel, splays his flanks.

Gingerly he's unhooked from his embrace
and the left stirrup. The gun-horse –
mane down over its confusion
of muzzles – maintains dressage balance

and poses the usual problem for the Detail.
Steak-stripped since the shell burst,
the last consummation's been had of it.
There's no petrol, a wood fire won't take.

Even clay, after some debate, and much
struggle toward the ditch, rejects its frame.
A week of repeat salvos – the parapet's
weak soil flensed to an equine shrapnel.

In Clitheroe Keep (I)

The point was still to hold the pass, control
the pack-horses' route over the Pennines

– thus, Clitheroe. Up on its hill-spur. Small
infringement, herald of a bad time

like the taxman's strongbox on arrival
slung above the stirrups, half a wind chime,

a bright wind, marching east for Pendle hill;
a sinew below its heather-coat of mail.

Clitheroe. A rest home, heroes in choky,
the climate and recline of locked-up kings

bookmarked as if bored by their own stories.
Clitheroe in air, spring's chilblain kind

or callous devils, cast in the scitter-tourney
or called time hourly to its witching song,

a bright wind-marching, east for Pendle hill;
a sinew below its heather-coat of mail

the slick hauberk of rain and a Lancs. postcode
the box of weather, a clear fill and reload

barely keepsake by the re-pointing of stones
by wind, by everything else that's just coming, just gone.

In Clitheroe Keep (II)

All wars are civil wars.
And so too, Lancashire
shared that before-diaspora

parcelling of the family:
the Whalleys of Whalley,
Foulridge, Bolton-By-

Bowland, its wet trough
gurgling suns. The troth
lines that the wind cuffs

from the headstones there:
my grandmother's grandmother
and the stillborn child with her.

You think always in foreign
English, the uncomforting
syllables lost to the tongue.

Clitheroe re-runs our kid's old news:
who's kept it up, who's moved
away, and on. Time's groove

like the dent left on your side
of the double bed; one line:
Ribble, Mons, Irrawaddy, Rhine.

It is true Rupert's cavaliers
and the prince himself gazetted here
en route to Marston Moor.

In Clitheroe Keep he barracked.

The Guinea Pig Club

That gaze, following days as though each were a dream;
one eye's bleary watercolour cobalt.
Patches of pale scrub skirting the embouchure.
A top lip thinned up over the denture seam.

One eye is bleary watercolour cobalt,
one eye painted lapis lazuli, just retouched.
A top lip thinned up over the denture seam
that will, in time, be trained to deploy smiles.

One eye painted lapis lazuli, just replaced
with a closer shade, a flighty blue-grey slate
that will, in time, be trained to reply smiles.
Three ageless lines for where they were put back together.

Much later, clean shaved, dressed in their blue-grey suits
in the longed-for pub, flirting. The embouchures
try ageless lines once more: "Shall we be together?"
and the gaze, that follows you night after night into dreams.

Caractacus in the Rape of Bramber

A tree-fall peels the scab of the pillbox fresh
and Britain is real again, brick red, a bargain
struck off the back of an overblown beach landing.

You know it by your tokens and your resistance,
even as the wind runs its hands through the rape
of Bramber, Wilberforce's rotten borough,
as through the hair of a lost child not its own;
as each search-light is the point of a comb's tooth.

If you go down to the woods, look in the woodshed,
get into a strange car, you'll find your narrator.
I, Caractacus - cut cold from Cymbeline
my father's side and left to fend off invaders -
am looking for children. *Pardon's the word to all.*
I'm hieing to Sussex, to sites of precedent.

King John took the kids from Bramber Castle,
dug the bailey's teeth out and starved the children.
Since the keep broke, after the Act of Union,
the children were heard to come home, play again
in the shadow of the one last upright wall;
as vast a shelter as the charter of John's crime.

In your night sweats, after the fuck, it's their hunger you feel
and John's and the castle's and mine, Caractacus,
exposing myself as a party to this fraud,
the nostalgia for an age of uniform fear,
a longing that hums in 'Moonlight Serenade'
which Morse's Jaguar came to consummate.

Ignore these warnings, if the hillforts tell you to do so,
if the tumuli mark you with their special font.
Take your firstborn and show them the market town-squares;
finger the pillories with them, teach them about garderobes,
mumble along in the flint-knapped grapeshot of Brythonic.

Give them these inches - then they'll take this, your country,
right down to its doggers' fissures, its Jermyn blight,
and up to its iliac crest, the sleek hips of the Downs.

Mink

Down the flooded season, down through swept
grasses to the puckered banks, the mink slipped
and was gone, without so much a splash

as blood that pelts out through the first jaw-grip
of pleasure-kills. The joy bandies its stench
as passport to the tributaries' riches.

How did the river feel to have the sunk
muscle and hair caught in its voiceless throat?
Or the mink, its nothing-to-answer-for coat
slick to the rippled silence of its back?

Only a feral noise would come, much later
when we, snug in the trim of privilege,
my tongue already tired, likened it
to how you might hear screaming underwater.

Concerning Plunder

On your coccyx, a gold contusion
holds the sinews, rope-braid tarred
to the treasure-ship of
your listing body.

I hurry to kiss it,
with the old piracy
woven into us
before torques were ravelled.

My not-ancestors, the White Rajahs
gave Sarawak a gold-fielded ensign;
but it never turned
to an honest Gibraltar.

I plant my kisses
above your arse
to the crack of your
terra nullius.

I've seen the blueprint of the slave ship *Brookes*,
the cargo in its wooden gut
is at least in part
my inheritance.

And this house that holds
seven tenths of my life
could never own me,
though the hold stays tight

as my roving dog
with a stick in his mouth
loosed on the fields
forgives my horror

that the branch in his maw
like a spar or a mast
is the still fur-clad
foreleg of a deer,

a leg that once sailed
in a whole perfect craft
never threatening to spill
its slight ingots of bone.

Surfeit

What a length of gut is growing and breathing
Ted Hughes

An eel-net made by man for the eel-fighting
Robert Lowell

Cry to it, nuncle, as the cockney did to the eels when she put 'em i'th'paste alive
Lear's Fool

Peel the silk-stocking skin back,
no-one escapes the gleaning of such a net,
feel the muscles
of history's peristalsis.
What haunts is inconspicuous, like hunger:
the eel's inner jaw, the lamprey's kiss.

Here's where the search for long-lost relatives
yields mixed results;
secondhand law books, mint minus.
Name one who unpicked themselves, could stomach
the anarchy, the unattributed comments,
sock puppetry, thread necromancy, lulls,
persistent myths of Greek flame, fuckwittery.

This ultima ratio regum was old meme
before the Good Clerk clicked checkout.
Still there's no stopping
reputations needing to be upheld,
justice, fair dealing,
the last appeal before
death's perpetual slander, the mute eater
thrashing against the curd of his own rennet.

Hydra

Evil is fissiparous – JRR Tolkein

Mustard – in gas, Dad? For evil is silly.
Like the summer of 1991,
when Dad was put on call for casualties
arriving at Gatwick. Our summer reading
at the age of obvious monsters, the ones that smell
fear, the blistering agents, the ones that get in
where you sweat. The ones that split cells.
The summer that we finished Lord of the Rings
and learned the difference between sarin and ricin.

Ordeal by Fire, By Water

i.m. Ambulance Driver Slater

War-time dark. Hedgerows through slatted headlights,
your ambulance convoy negotiating B roads.
And one of the two in the back is a burns case -
the worst kind, will not quiet – the other, you'd have him
up with you for his eyes alone -
                but his breath clouds the windscreen.

You've missed out on France: were ice-skating
on the billet's pond, feel through the thin roof
into that unreal house of darkness beamed
by frozen branches, skirt billowing just
as it did when you, a child, caught
                a loose coal from the grating.

Water the most dark, blacker still than water
at Balham tube when you were first on scene.
The silence as it was then, with the limbs.
Somehow, hands pulled you out. Into the night
you went dancing, like this patient
                who quick-stepped with a squadron's

petrol ration. Each moment's a test
or gift. Now the van stalls. Now ignition.
Now ice shudders from the upright exhaust.

Diastole

Submarine Chief Petty Officer Usher on shore leave at Trincomalee c.1941

Your stomach has settled.
You have slept in your trousers and watch
your knife hand now as through a periscope –
a ring finger, a thumb,
a rushed breakfast you slurp to the dregs.
Tea scummed with milk powder
spreads dark to the edge of its saucer.
Below and beneath
the flag of sunk shadow unfurls itself.

The waitress' pincered finger finesses the cork out
with a minimal fuss of vapour.
She blinks; you eye her.
The fogged champagne trickles,
a voice calls you for a yard of ale.
The ballast tanks flushed and you have saved them all.

Chunks of white brown
romp under the jetty
that's your thighbone, mouldrite,
the sump of an engine. *We lost*
Singapore of course because all our guns
were pointing at the sea.

Water rushes in to candle the dying
room with short-out voltages, glugged gasps
of brine steam, bilge soot.
Your mind shrinks from the cold,
your skull's bulwarks
drum to it.
To lose a ship! The fused plates
strain at their sutures.
Again, you press your thumbnail to the button's socket.

Silent Enim Leges Inter Arma

While Flying Officer Brookes is put on a charge
for negligent loss of cargo, the wounded Gurkha
Rifles step away safely under guard

as witnesses from a plane made happily lighter:
still a full complement of parachutes,
but a deficit of Japanese prisoners –

there was a short detention, then a release.

Two Seasons for the Tees-Exe Line

Growing mere graft, myrrh,
more roads, grist and rage.

Grey moats the sky, greets
migrants. Mist goads

glared mirth. Myths and graves.
Moors; the sleet mints groats.

God grant us meet minds,
manner grief. Give. Save.

        §

Gorse, yellowhammers,
weltering treasures.

Gallows of hawthorn
warding the glebe-land.

Good torrified wheat,
warped hopes, gelding tools,

galled thrush-worried hamlets:
Wicken Bonhunt. Wendens Ambo.

Notes

The Sweating Sickness, also known as 'The English Sweate' (sudor anglicus) was the name given to a highly virulent disease, first recorded in England in 1485 when Thomas Stanley, 1st Earl of Derby used the "sweating sickness" as an excuse not to join with Richard III's army prior to the Battle of Bosworth Field. Unusually for the time, the disease seems to have been more virulent among the rich than the poor. The last known outbreak occurred in 1552, after which it apparently vanished. The cause and subsequent disappearance of the disease remains unexplained.

Caractacus, son of Cunobelius (or Cymbeline), an ancient king of Britain, led the resistance against the Claudian invasion of AD43. Eventually captured and brought to Rome for execution as part of a triumphal parade, he was however allowed to address the Senate, who pardoned and released him. *Pardon's the word to all* is taken from Shakespeare's Cymbeline, in which the character of Caractacus does not appear.

The epigraph taken from Harry Peacham's Emblem 75 translates as 'purity bought with its own death'. Renaissance legend had it that the hunted ermine would turn and give itself up rather than soil its own coat. *Isti mirant stella* ('they marvel at the star') was woven into the Bayeux tapestry by English women, depicting a heavenly sign of approval for William the Bastard's invasion.

In 'The Crescent of Hearing', the italicised text on the sentence of the Prynne, Burton and Bastwicke, 30 June 1637 is taken from an account found in John Rushworth (1706, abridged edition) Historical Collections volume two, pp. 293. The Captain Jenkins mentioned in '1737' was Robert Jenkins, captain of a British merchant ship, which was boarded by Spanish coast guards in 1731 who severed the ear he would later exhibit in Parliament.

The 'Rape of Bramber' is one of the traditional sub-divisions of Sussex and a former barony granted by William the Conqueror to William de Braose, who built the castle. His descendant, also a William, was a favourite of King John. They quarreled after John killed his nephew Prince Arthur in a drunken temper – William refused to hand over his sons as surance of loyalty; John seized the de Braose possessions and imprisoned William's wife and sons at Windsor and then Corfe in Devon, where they starved to death five years before Magna Carta.

'The Guinea Pig' was a drinking club formed by the WWII patients, many of them airmen, who underwent reconstructive plastic surgery at the Queen Victoria Hospital, East Grinstead, Sussex.

In 'Concerning Plunder', the 'blueprint' referred to is the poster 'Stowage of the British Slave Ship *Brookes* Under the Regulated Slave Trade Act of 1788', first designed in Plymouth, England in 1788 by the Plymouth Chapter of the Society for Effecting the Abolition of the Slave Trade.

Henry I, called 'Beauclerc' for his scholarly nature and legal reforms, died after reportedly eating a 'surfeit of lampreys', precipitating a succession crisis and nineteen years of internecine conflict popularly known as 'the Anarchy'.

'Silent Enim Leges Inter Arma' is from Cicero's oration *Pro Milone*: 'for the laws are mute in times of war'.

All narratives concerning members of my family during the Second World War appear as reported to me first, second or third hand. Events have thus been conflated, displaced from their chronological sequence and context or otherwise adapted until only the most enduring and necessary fictions remain.

Acknowledgements

Acknowledgements are due to the Society of Authors for an Eric Gregory Award and to the editors of the following publications in which these poems first appeared: 'Shrike', 'Mons Horse Burial', 'In Clitheroe Keep (I)' and 'In Clitheroe Keep (II)' in Horizon Review; 'The Crescent of Hearing' in The Warwick Review; an early version of 'Two Seasons for the Tees-Exe Line' (titled 'Englynd') online at Gists&Piths.blogspot.com.

My thanks to George Ttoouli, Michael Hulse and all at the Warwick Writing Programme; to Fiona Sampson and to Peter and Amanda Carpenter for advice and employment; to Alex Carruth and Tom Boardman for lending their eyes. My deepest thanks to my family and to Charlotte Newman.

My particular thanks to David Morley, Peter Longshaw and Christopher StJohn Perry, sine quibus non.

James Brookes was born in 1986 and has lived in Sussex for most of the last 20 years. He studied at the University of Warwick and has been Senior Student Editor, then a Contributing Editor of The Warwick Review. His work has appeared in various places, including Poetry Review, Horizon Review, the Swedish journal Signum and on a church pew in Taunton, Somerset. In 2009 he received an Eric Gregory Award from the Society of Authors.